Peaceful Mind/Peaceful Life:

The Guidebook to Happiness

Dr. Steven Davidson

drstevendavidson.com

Peaceful Mind/Peaceful Life: The Guidebook to Happiness

Dr. Steven Davidson

drstevendavidson.com

All rights reserved. No part of this book may be reproduced or transmitted in any form or by any means, electronic or mechanical, including photocopying, recording, or by any information storage and retrieval system without the permission of the publisher.

Disclaimer

This book is not intended as a substitute for psychotherapy, coaching, or counseling, nor should it be used to diagnose or treat any medical or psychological condition. The reader should consult a physician or therapist in matters related to personal health. This book is intended to provide information and education to the reader. Neither the author, the editors, nor the publisher shall be held liable for any physical, psychological, emotional, relational, financial, or spiritual outcomes. The case scenarios in this book are based on real situations though the names and all personal identifying information have been altered to protect identity.

First Printing: 2023

Published by ManWitch Productions

Wilton Manors, FL

www.themanwitch.com

Copyright © 2023 by Steven Davidson

First Edition

ISBN 978-1-7373397-3-1

Library of Congress Control Number 2023907916

DEDICATION

In memory of Edna Estelle Davidson
(Memaw)

Thank you for modeling a peaceful life.

Table of Contents

Chapter One : In Pursuit of Happiness 1

Chapter Two : The Enemy Within 9

Chapter Three : Making Peace 17

Chapter Four : All the World Is a Stage 26

Chapter Five : Changing It.. 31

Chapter Six : Leaving It... 36

Chapter Seven : Accepting It!.. 44

Chapter Eight : Mastering Thoughts.............................. 50

Chapter Nine : Mastering Emotions 58

Chapter Ten : Taking Action... 66

Chapter Eleven : The Role of Faith 76

Chapter Twelve : Getting Help... 83

Chapter Thirteen : Take Aways.. 90

About the Author.. 102

Chapter One

In Pursuit of Happiness

Why does happiness seem so illusive? We look for it in people and find ourselves disappointed and broken-hearted. We look for it in things, but landfills and thrift stores are full of the things we once believed we couldn't live without. Our social media accounts highlight our travels, accomplishments, and celebrations, yet in reality, we struggle to find real purpose in day-to-day life. We are all actors portraying characters other than ourselves. What if we stopped acting and started living? Instead of looking elsewhere for happiness, what if we looked within?

David did everything right. In childhood, teachers commented on what a good boy he was. He was studious and obedient and got along well with others. He was active in his church youth group and the Boy Scouts. He played in a softball league during the summer and a volleyball league in the winter. He had a college scholarship and graduated with honors.

After college David landed a job in finance and began saving money for his first home, he married his college sweetheart; Anna, and they had their first child two years later. He mowed the lawn, washed and waxed the car, took out the trash, bought flowers for Anna on their anniversary and Valentine's Day, called his mom on the weekends, went to work on time, volunteered for charity, and wore the company logo on his polo shirt with starched khakis on casual Friday. "Such a nice guy," everyone said. David was the golden boy.

In therapy, David complains about his boring life. He feels confused because he has followed the rules but isn't happy. Inside David feels dead. He hates his job, but it distracts him from thinking about how miserable he is otherwise. When he gets in his car in the evening to drive home, he starts to feel nausea, his heart races, and he perspires. These were the symptoms he took to his physician, who diagnosed him with anxiety and referred him to a therapist. On the surface, it all looked good, but deep inside, David was seething with anger, self-loathing, and unhappiness with his life. The facade was crumbling, and David was about to deal with the truth.

We are all groomed to live in the world we are born into. We don't all get the same chances. We don't get to choose where we grow up or who we grow up with. We don't get to choose our genetics or the culture we are socialized in. In the beginning, there were many decisions someone else made for us, and often they made bad choices or chose for us what they wanted for themselves. No matter how hard we try, we just can't fit into the box we were given. It's uncomfortable and awkward, and smiling through the agony leaves us feeling disconnected and alone.

Certain themes come up in therapy repeatedly, human themes related to our quest for purpose, fulfillment, and happiness. Sometimes it shows up as depression, and sometimes anxiety. We might self-medicate with alcohol or drugs. The solution is not out there. It is within your own mind, and you have to search within yourself to discover your own path to happiness. How do you do that? You are about to find out.

Right now, can you honestly say you are living your best life? Is this the life you dreamed of? Are you living in the moment, or are you trapped in the past, unable to let go and move on? Do you constantly worry about what could go wrong next? Does fear of the unpredictable future prevent you from chasing your dreams and trying something new? Do you have everything you wanted, but it isn't bringing you joy?

This book goes straight to the core of the problems people bring to therapy. It gives practical solutions for coping with our cognitive and emotional reactions to life's challenges, big and small. This is your opportunity to take control of your life. You will discover what is changeable and how to change it. You will gain clarity regarding when it is time to walk away. You will also discover the value of acceptance of those things that can't be changed, and for whatever reason, you will not leave behind.

David

David felt dead inside because he had never lived his own life. Someone was always talking him out of what he wanted. He hated sports. He played volleyball and softball as a compromise with his father, who insisted he should play football. David really wanted to learn music and play in the band. In childhood, he wanted violin lessons, but his dad insisted he should join the Scouts. David hated his job in finance. His dad encouraged this career because it was a path to financial security. He loved Anna and his daughter, but marriage came way too early. David felt like a younger version of his father, which terrified him. He didn't know where to begin to look for himself.

In therapy, David realized he needed to grieve the time he lost. What was in the past could not be changed, but he didn't have to bring it into his present and future life. Gradually he deconstructed the life his dad had insisted on and built the life that gave him joy. His anxiety began to subside as he became more aware of his true desires and allowed himself to pursue them. He took violin lessons and swapped his starched khakis for jeans. He left his corporate position for a finance director job with a non-profit organization that helps inner-city children. He and Anna moved from the suburbs to a trendy community in the city. Within five years, David felt like he was truly living his life and not his dad's. He slept better. He laughed more. Anna even found him a little sexier. He had transformed his life by changing the things standing in his way of happiness.

Elena

Elena and Gail met in their thirties through mutual friends. They fell in love quickly and Gail moved in with Elena four months after they met. The first few years were fast and fun. They partied hard on weekends and recovered through the week. As time passed, Elena felt she couldn't keep pace with Gail. Elena wanted to slow down, but Gail insisted she keep up. On weekends Elena began faking illness in hopes they would stay home. It worked the first time, but the second time Gail went out without her. By their fourth year, Elena was staying home most weekends while Gail maintained her partying pace.

When Gail was arrested for driving under the influence (DUI), Elena hoped that would slow her down. She regretted the arrest but thought this would convince Gail to stay home and drink less. If anything, Gail drank more. She took a taxi, she walked, and a few times, she even hitched, a practice that made Elena worry more about Gail's safety.

Five years in, Gail lost her job. She told Elena there were company layoffs due to economics, but Elena suspected Gail's drinking played a role. Elena confronted Gail and insisted she get help for her alcohol abuse. Gail accused Elena of not being supportive. She told Elena that she had changed since they met. "What happened, Elena? You used to be so much fun."

Elena went to therapy alone because Gail refused to go. She told the therapist everything she had tried to get Gail to stop drinking. None of them worked. The DUI, the lost job, and the relationship problems didn't seem to affect Gail's attitude or behavior. Elena was now paying all their bills, driving Gail to appointments, and spending her weekends home alone while Gail partied and did whatever else she wanted to do.

Therapy helped Elena see that her present problem was not her own doing. Elena was holding herself and Gail up because Gail had relinquished all accountability for her behavior and circumstances. "You can't fix Gail's drinking problem," the therapist explained. "You only have power over yourself. Your options are to live with it or to leave it. Only Gail can determine when she is ready to change her life." She recommended Elena go to Al-Anon and gave her a brochure.

Elena thought about the therapist's statements. It was hard to believe there was nothing she could do to change Gail's behavior. In Al-Anon, Elena learned she had to accept her powerlessness over Gail's addiction and the necessity that she save herself. It took another year, but Elena decided to leave her relationship with Gail. She couldn't change Gail's behavior. She couldn't accept Gail's drinking and the ongoing stress this placed on her life. However, she could leave and start over somewhere else. She loved Gail and she worried about her, but she loved herself enough to leave.

Carolyn and Jack

"For better or worse, until death do us part." Those were their vows when Carolyn and Jack were married. Marriage was serious for Carolyn. It was a holy union binding a couple in love for eternity. It was serious for Jack too. He loved Carolyn and had no intention of leaving her. However, he could not claim fidelity. Jack had cheated on Carolyn multiple times and she was not sure she could ever trust him again.

The couple had avoided therapy. They went to their pastor for guidance on such personal matters. The pastor coached Carolyn on humility and forgiveness. He coached Jack on repentance and avoiding temptations of the flesh. This reinforced the couple's faith in God, but Carolyn could not get over Jack's betrayal and deceit. Trusting him again was something she was not sure she could ever do, no matter how hard she tried. Laying under him in bed repulsed her now, yet she feared he would betray her again if she did not.

Carolyn cried most days. She had anger outbursts at Jack. Jack got angry in return and Carolyn cried more. Each time they attempted sex Carolyn would break into tears and run from the room. They conceded to therapy when they both agreed they could not go on like this. "Divorce is not an option," Carolyn insisted. "If the therapist tells us to divorce, I am not going back."

For Jack, the therapy moved too slowly. He wanted faster results, yet things at home seemed to change very little. For Carolyn, she found the therapist to be patient and supportive. She felt validated for her feelings and didn't feel pushed to pretend that none of this had happened or to divorce Jack and move on. The therapist affirmed that Carolyn's feelings were legitimate. Jack's past behavior had caused her to distrust him and fear he would repeat his betrayal. After all, it had happened more than once.

Progress for couples like Carolyn and Jack does not come quickly. Some couples will not survive the fallout that results from infidelity. If acceptance is not achievable, divorce will be the choice for many couples in this situation. The past cannot be changed and the deception that has transpired will always throw doubt on the future. That is a heavy burden to carry whether you are the cheated or the cheater. Faith was the necessary ingredient for Carolyn since her past with Jack could not be changed, and she would not allow herself to leave.

For over thirty-five years, I have worked in the field of mental health; in psychiatric hospitals, outpatient family service clinics, and my own psychotherapy practice. As a licensed psychotherapist, clinical sexologist, and personal coach, I have provided services in some capacity to thousands of individuals. I have seen patients in individual, couple, family, and group psychotherapy. I have seen every diagnosis in the book. Every problem brought to therapy lies in one or more of three places in time: the past, the present, or the future. With every problem, we have three options: change it, leave it, or accept it. Start here. Where does your problem reside? What are your options? This is the foundation of beginning to plan for your peaceful mind, your peaceful life, and your own path to happiness.

The practical tools in this book make it simple to assess your thoughts and feelings and choose a reasonable solution. You will learn skills to deal with many of life's challenges that impede your pursuit of happiness. If you use these tools, you will learn how to put your mind at peace and create and maintain a peaceful life. These are the skills I teach my clients. Are you ready?

Chapter Two

The Enemy Within

We are interesting and complex creatures. Throughout the history of humanity, we have made the same mistakes repeatedly. Collectively we never learn. While knowledge evolves, human behavior does not. Humankind remains driven by greed, anger, lust, desire, and power. We are ego-centered creatures with little capacity for empathy for the global community. We see this in every culture throughout the known history of humankind. We strive for civilization, but it is against our nature. Like every other creature, we are innately wired to survive and thrive no matter who we must harm to do it. There are sufficient resources to feed, clothe, shelter, and provide healthcare for every human on this earth, but humans have never collectively taken care of each other. Anthropologists and sociologists doubt we ever will. The world is not a peaceful place. As much as we all wish for world peace, we have never achieved it. Humans are constantly at battle with each other personally, politically, and globally. We cannot be at peace with each other until we are at peace with ourselves.

At age sixty-two, William was a lonely, angry man. He had been divorced from Emily for nineteen years and never remarried. He had dated a few times after the divorce, but it never worked out well for him. He had two grown children who had not spoken to him in several years. He had a grandchild he had never seen. He said he didn't care; it was their loss.

Each day after work, William would go to a local pub for dinner and a few beers. He would occasionally start a conversation with someone at the bar, but he frequently offended people with his commentary on the state of world affairs. The bartender was the only consistent person who talked to him, and he didn't really have a choice.

William didn't take responsibility for any of the unfortunate outcomes in his life. The way he tells it, he was right. It was his wife, his children, the president—"those people." They were all to blame for everything that had ever gone wrong in William's life. William had done a lot of things right. He served his country in the military for four years. He worked hard and never asked anyone to pay his way. He voted, paid his taxes, never robbed a bank, or shot anyone. He had a cross tattooed on his left arm and an American flag on his right. He loved his country and was proud of that. So why is this man who did it all right so angry and alone?

William had high expectations of himself and everyone else. People rarely measured up to his expectations. He had no tolerance for anyone who didn't see it his way. He had his own definition of success and measured everyone else by the same metric. He was acting from the script he was given early in his life. His father was a strong-willed authoritarian who believed children should be seen and not heard. He cut young William no slack and insisted he would make a man out of him. William was told to follow his dad's instructions and he would be a success. In many ways, William had succeeded, but not in the ways that caused people to stay in his life. He could not celebrate the successes of others if their achievements did not measure up to his assumptions about how life should be.

William wasn't empathetic to the struggles of others. He segregated people into categories of good and bad, right and wrong. This process had become so automatic that he wasn't consciously aware he was doing it. It was all happening in his head according to the rules in his mind. Even his own family had not passed his inspection.

William preferred the company of those who shared his beliefs. This helped him feel vindicated and entitled to never re-evaluate his attitude and opinions. He insulated himself from ideas that would challenge his own world view. Life was serious business and everyone he met was a potential threat.

William had been given multiple opportunities to free himself from his mental prison, but he believed that would be settling for less than he deserved. He remained committed to making his dad proud though he was now deceased. William refused to accept that the world was not as he believed it should be. He preferred his beliefs over his family and now he was alone. He wanted to make friends at the neighborhood pub, but people avoided him because of his toxic personality. In a few years, he would retire, and his only aspiration was to spend his days in his recliner watching the news. He would feed his head with more stories to support his position that the world had gone to hell.

Emily, William's ex-wife, divorced William when she had given up hope of ever having the relationship with him she so desired. She had begged him to get counseling with her, but he refused. "It's your problem," he said. "I don't have a problem. Get therapy for yourself." So, she did. In therapy, Emily examined why she ever dated William and why she said yes to his marriage proposal. It seems Emily had traded her own critical father for a critical husband. She had perceived William's behavior to be indicative of confidence and authority. She now thought of it as immaturity, bullying, and bordering abuse. When she realized how her father's behavior had negatively influenced her choices in life, she knew she had to get her children away from the influence of William. So, she decided to leave and take the children with her.

The children had regular visitation with William. He was consistent with child support and spending time with them. He likely made the best effort he could, but he could not connect with them emotionally. He was critical, judgmental, shaming, and sometimes verbally abusive. After visitations, the children often returned to Emily sad, angry, and begging not to return to their father's home again. When Emily tried to discuss this with William, he told her that he had rules and that the children would follow his rules under his roof. By late adolescence, the children were simply refusing to see their father. Instead of trying to mend the relationship, William dug in his heels. He told them he would complete the payments of his child support, but beyond that, he was done.

Today Emily is happily married to another man. She has regular contact with her two children and her grandchild. They are a close family who support and encourage each other. When she reflects on her marriage to William, she feels proud that she took the initiative to leave a bad situation and change her life in ways that made her and her children happier and healthier individuals. She feels sad for William when she thinks about him growing old alone and so disconnected from his family. However, she accepts that William is a grown man with a right to make his own choices, even if they are not in his best interest.

Though William believed he was in control of his life, he was making decisions that ultimately harmed himself. Early on, he formed rigid beliefs about how the world should be. He did the things he assumed would earn him respect but found himself alone. He had rigid expectations of others and often felt disappointed. He judged everyone by the rules he had created for himself, and no one measured up to be worthy of his time. His ego could not tolerate the possibility that he was wrong. He wouldn't allow his mind to believe that maybe his father's opinions were not necessarily facts. He carried them in his heart and mind like he was guarding a precious stone. He would not allow himself to learn something new. He denied himself opportunities to expand his world and actively worked to keep it small. He would not change his mind. He would not accept that he was responsible for his own consequences. His mind was not at peace, which was reflected throughout his life. William was not happy.

Ironically, we are often our own worst enemy. We judge ourselves more harshly than anyone else. We sabotage our own success. We hold onto beliefs that stopped serving us a long time ago, if ever. Many of our beliefs are inherited from someone else. They are not even original thoughts. Your religion, politics, traditions, and habits are influenced by others, some of whom died a long time ago.

We are gullible and impressionable. We learn as children to trust our elders and respect their authority. This goes well when the adults in our life are healthy, compassionate, intelligent human beings. Under their guidance, we can grow into independent adults able to individuate with confidence. Under the influence of those driven by power and greed, we are groomed to dissociate from our own thoughts and desires and judge them as evil. The unhealthy thoughts and beliefs are integrated, and we are no longer individually recognizable. We are committed to the problem and refuse the solution. We are not happy because we are not ourselves.

Our minds are wired to defend our bodies so we can survive and evolve individually and as a species. The evolving mind can't distinguish the body from ego or a physical threat from a conceptual threat, so it fights everyone and everything. It looks for other like-minded creatures to claim as its tribe. It wants to reinforce itself against the perceived enemy even though the real enemy resides within. We must intentionally override the innate and learned barriers to our happiness. This is necessary if we are to ever be at peace.

Even in therapy, we see clients' resistance to change. They came because they wanted to feel better, yet they cling to the exact people, places, and habits that reinforce their emotional pain. They may judge it is too late, too risky, or too uncertain to do something different, so they keep doing what they have always done, wishing for a different outcome.

Right now can be the beginning of change. Right now is an opportunity to try a different route in your pursuit of happiness. Right now is a great time to surrender those thoughts and beliefs that hold you back and replace them with new thoughts that will lead you to success. After all, most of our perceived reality is nothing more than thought. Thought was the foundation of every religion. Thoughts are the principles that form every nation. Channeled thought is the mission of every university as it graduates specialists in every field. It is thought that defines the world and dictates the actions that lead to happiness or misery. Thoughts influence emotions, which influence the choices we make and the actions we take.

William and Emily are examples of two individuals who grew up in very similar situations. They found each other in their common thoughts. While William never changed his mind, Emily did. She recognized she was unhappy, and she did something about it. She saw that her children were on a bleak path forward, and so she changed their course. She discovered that what she had been told about life, relationships, and the world was not bringing her happiness, so she let herself think different thoughts and take different actions. She accepted her past. She left the people and places that brought her pain. She changed her life in a way that brought her peace.

When she looked within, she didn't blame others. She held herself accountable for staying stuck in situations that obstructed her path to happiness.

Chapter Three

Making Peace

This is not the first book about happiness, and it will not be the last. We, humans, are slow learners when it comes to making personal changes. We have to read the same information again and again. New clients sometimes come to therapy and ask how long it will take to get over their depression, anxiety, and grief. "How many sessions will it take to make my marriage better?" That is up to you. Some readers of this book will start making changes immediately. Others will read ten books on happiness and do absolutely nothing different. A broken leg, on average, heals in six to eight weeks. A broken heart sometimes never heals, and a mind in chaos sometimes never finds peace.

You may already be familiar with many of the basic principles of happiness. None of them work if you don't apply them. You must be proactive at seeking peace within. You must stop looking to other people, places, or things in search of joy. Each of us is on a solo journey. No one else is walking in your shoes, living in your body, or navigating the thoughts in your head. It's up to you.

Somewhere in Time:

Life's problems fall within three places in time: the past, the present, or the future. We want to fix something that has already happened or is happening to us right now. We want to settle our minds about something from the past. We want to resolve a problem we are experiencing today. Problems cannot exist in the future because the future has not yet happened. You can certainly worry about the future, but you are worrying in the present.

Past:

The past is behind you. It has already happened. It is not changeable. The only thing you can change is your attitude about it and the conclusions you came to regarding what it means about you in the present. There are some traumas we can resolve and move on from. There are others from which we never fully recover. Horrible things happened in our past that influence how we think about ourselves in the present. With the diagnosis of Post Traumatic Stress Disorder (PTSD), the patient has brought the past trauma into the present and continues to live life as if the trauma is still occurring in the moment. There are interventions therapists use to help patients move through the trauma and leave it in the past. It is not forgotten, but it no longer impedes the patient's happiness in the present and future. We can't change what happened in the past, but we can change what we think about it.

Present:

The present is where the magic happens. Some say that time is just an illusion and that right now is all that exists. Physicists and philosophers have weighed in on the subject with mind-blowing theories and concepts. Psychologically, humans understand time linearly based on our own experiences of life. Planet earth is estimated to be over 4.5 billion years old. Your life isn't even a recognizable dot in the universe, but it matters to you, so claim it and make the best of it.

For the focus of this book, I maintain that the past is a memory, and the future is a fantasy. They are simply thoughts that evoke emotion and influence our perception of ourselves. It is right now in the present where change happens. This is where your opportunity for happiness resides. Every moment is an opportunity to think a better thought and choose a better course of action. Right now is a great time to change the outcome of your future.

Future:

It is right to plan for the future while living in the present. Right now is an ideal time to save money for tomorrow. Right now, you can start training for the career you will have in five years. Everything you want tomorrow is made possible by the choices you make today.

However, it can get tricky. So many of life's big events (good and bad) are never planned. You never know who you will meet and how they will significantly influence your life. You never know what disasters will come tomorrow that could dramatically change your experience of the future. The pandemic of 2020 is a great example. We didn't see it coming; it has changed our lives individually and collectively.

Staying stuck in the past can lead to depression. It weighs us down. If we continue to judge ourselves in the present based on events from the past, we may experience resentment, regrets, grief, guilt, or shame. We fail to see the present as a new opportunity. We go through life looking in the rearview mirror, which impedes our ability to seize the opportunities given to us today. Our heart gets broken, and we declare that we will never love again. We fail in our pursuit of a dream and decide we will never try again. It is hard to not let life's disappointments crush our dreams and cause us to give up hope.

In every moment, we make the best possible decisions based on the information and resources we have at that moment. Life's lessons give us new information whereby we can continue to make better decisions in the future. When you look at the past with regret, you judge yourself from a different place. All of us have those life experiences where we might say, "If I knew then what I know now . . ." Well, you didn't know it then. The choices you made were based on your best judgment at that moment. Rarely does anyone set out to fuck it up. This would be contrary to our basic human instinct to survive and evolve. You likely gave it your best. Your best today will be even better.

Everything that has happened in your life thus far has brought you to where you are today. What judgments have you made about yourself? What conclusions about your life have you reached, and how are they serving you today? We can change our experience of life simply by changing our mind. Making peace with the past will change how you live in the present. How you live today will determine your level of happiness tomorrow.

The Three Options:

In every challenge in life, we have three options: change it, leave it, or accept it. It is empowering and confidence-building to actively change our circumstances for the better. Rarely does change come quickly, and almost always, it comes at a price. To have one thing, something else must be forfeited. To have a new car, one must forfeit the money to pay for it. To have more physical strength, one must forfeit time in their schedule to go to a gym. Some people avoid change because they don't want to forfeit the time, money, etc. it takes to achieve their dream.

Watching this is sad. It happens for many reasons. Sometimes a person just doesn't know where or how to begin. No one has ever shown them the path. Sometimes they don't have the financial resources or the personal connections to get them an equal chance at success. Sometimes they place others' needs before their own. They neglect their own needs to care for someone else out of love or perceived obligation.

Change It!

Our greatest potential for change lies close in. We have more influence over ourselves and our immediate surroundings than we do the rest of the world. Start with yourself. Make a list of the things you want to change in your life. Now pick just one thing on the list, even if it is small or easy. Identify what it would take to accomplish it. Time? Money? A phone call? Set a realistic deadline that you can achieve. The goal here is to win. You need to experience in any small way what it feels like to succeed at changing something in your life. It's empowering. Now move your way through the rest of the list.

What if I change it and it doesn't work out? Then you can change it again. Remember that the future is not known. Every action in life is potentially risky. It's just that some are riskier than others. Staying stuck and doing nothing might be the greatest risk of all. If what you are currently doing brings you happiness, then there likely is no good reason to change it. Happiness is what we are striving for.

Leave It!

Many of us grew up learning that we should never give up. "Don't be a quitter." "Finish what you start." "Stick to your promises." Mostly this is good advice unless your situation is making you sick. It's okay to change your mind. It's okay to recognize that you no longer want the thing you once chose; the job, the relationship, the life. If you can change it for the better, then do so. Couples see therapists to avoid ending the relationship and to make the relationship more accommodating to the needs of the individuals involved. Jobs can be more fulfilling if the salary is right, the hours are convenient, and the responsibilities are reasonable, but these situations are not up to you alone. You need the cooperation of your spouse, your boss, or someone else so you can make the changes that will allow you to stay. Change is easiest when we don't need to rely on anyone else. When others do not allow change to happen, we sometimes have to leave.

Accept It!

Humans have a tenacious capacity for tolerating misery. It is part of our innate drive to survive. In every moment, we decide how we will survive another day. Sometimes we decide that change is necessary for survival. Sometimes we decide our best means of survival is leaving our situation. Not everything can be either changed or left behind. Some things can only be accepted if we are to recover and move on.

Acceptance is under-rated. Like changing it and leaving it, acceptance is also a viable option. It is a decision to live with what is. That itself is a form of change. You change your mind about the situation you cannot change otherwise.

You are the CEO in your own life. If no one else treats you fairly, at least treat yourself. Make the executive decisions you need to make about what you will change, what you will leave, and what you are willing to accept.

Our Five Senses:

We perceive the world through our five senses of sight, sound, taste, smell, and touch. They are the basis of how we receive data input and form thoughts, beliefs, and opinions. That looks pretty, sounds relaxing, tastes awesome, smells nasty, and feels great. Sensations are subjective. We don't all perceive the world the same way. What tastes awesome to one person can taste bad to another. What one finds pretty, another may find repulsive. Seventy degrees feels too cool to one and too warm to another. This is a great example of how the perception of life influences the extent to which we feel happy.

Conflicts can occur in relationships when our perceptions are not in synchronicity. Each person judges the other and approaches the relationship as if their perceptions were facts. There are many ways to perceive the same stimuli in the world. Sometimes all we need to change is our mind and accept the other person's right to be different.

Emotions:

Our perceptions of the world will drive our emotions. Like our senses, emotions are just feelings about our perceptions (thoughts). Not right or wrong. Arguing about emotions is as futile as arguing about our sensory perceptions because they are also subjective. One person might feel sad when it rains, while another feels joy. If we have the capacity to experience the same stimuli differently, then our perceptions of life are just our individual opinions about what is good or bad, right or wrong, or anywhere in between.

Emotions are abstract concepts that cannot be measured universally. We use different words to identify variations of the same emotion. Is *frustrated* different from *annoyed*? Both are variations of anger. People have difficulty identifying their emotions. They frequently confuse emotions with thoughts. They say things like, "I feel like you don't care about me," or "I feel like my opinion doesn't matter." These are thoughts that might evoke emotions of anger, sadness, or fear. People also confuse emotions with behavior. They deny feeling anger because they aren't yelling or punching anyone in the face. They deny feeling fear because they aren't trembling in tears. Yelling and trembling are actions that express emotions. They are not the emotion itself. We can't always determine what someone is feeling by judging how they behave.

We tend to project onto others our own experiences of life. We make assumptions about others based on our own opinions. Conflict occurs when others don't live up to our expectations or assumptions about right and wrong. When an individual doesn't behave according to another individual's opinion (thoughts), they might feel frustrated, annoyed, angry, sad, or afraid.

Peace and happiness are judgments about our status based on our perception of our life, just another opinion driven by thoughts and emotions. This is why it is so important that you claim responsibility for yourself. That you stop looking *out* and start looking *within*. That you don't allow others to define you, you define yourself. That you live in the present moment because it is the only place in time where you have any power or control.

Chapter Four

All the World Is a Stage

In 1980 Gina graduated from college. Her grandmother knew how much she loved the theatre, so she gave her a trip to New York as a graduation gift. Her hotel, airfare, and theatre tickets were paid for. Gina's parents gave her cash for meals and local transportation. Gina had been to New York with her parents a few times. She loved the fast vibe of the city. She always felt so glamorous visiting the places she had seen in movies and read about in books.

While in New York, Gina ate breakfast in the hotel diner each morning. She always had the same server, a beautiful young lady named Vanessa. The young women would chat as Vanessa poured coffee and cleaned the nearby tables in the diner. Gina explained that she was in town for a week as a graduation gift from her grandmother and that this was her first time in New

York by herself. Vanessa shared that she had lived in New York for a few years and moved there to chase her dream of being an actress on Broadway. She had several theatre friends and suggested that Gina join her at a cast party later that evening. Gina was so excited. She had only been in town a few days, and already the locals were inviting her to a party. What famous person might she meet?

That night Vanessa met Gina at the hotel and the two walked a few blocks to the party. The room was full of good-looking men and women who were young actors and dancers. None of them were famous, but they believed they were on their way. Vanessa introduced Gina to the guests she knew, including her friend Felipe. Felipe was a charming young man with handsome Latin features. He wasn't an actor, but he did work in the theatre on set design and maintenance. As soon as their eyes met, Gina felt herself fall in love.

By 1990 Gina and Felipe had been married seven years. They had one daughter, Maria. Gina was teaching school in Miami and Felipe had started a construction business specializing in kitchen renovations. Vanessa, who had been Gina's maid of honor at their wedding, was now living in Jersey City. She had given up on her dream of becoming an actress. She had a few small parts here and there and some modeling opportunities, but nothing consistently paid the bills. Vanessa was struggling to find her way now; she was not in a relationship and was unsure what she wanted to do with the rest of her life.

By 2010 so much had changed in Gina and Vanessa's lives. Gina and Felipe had been married for seventeen years. Maria, now fifteen years old, is thinking about college. Vanessa had been working for several years as an international flight attendant, and she married a pilot who worked for the same airline. They did not have children together, but he has a daughter, Annette, from a previous marriage, and she is the same age as Maria.

Felipe's business was doing well. As a Christmas gift to his family, he booked a cruise and invited Vanessa and her family to join. It was on this cruise that Maria and Annette met for the first time. The two girls became friends and agreed to stay in touch after the cruise.

In 2022 Gina flew to Seattle for Annette's wedding. She went alone because Felipe had died from a heart attack one year prior. Maria had lived in Seattle for several years and moved there to go to college at the University of Washington, where she and Annette were roommates. Maria would be the maid of honor at Annette's wedding. Vanessa and her husband, Maria's dad, would meet Gina in Seattle, where they stayed at the same hotel. On the morning of the wedding, Gina and Vanessa agreed to meet in the hotel diner for breakfast. They spoke about the changes in their lives now that their daughters were grown and Felipe had died. "I wonder what's next for us?" Vanessa said. "You just never know what the future will bring. What's it been, thirty years?" Gina asked. "I don't know," Vanessa replied. "I lose track of time."

A young waitress came to the table to refill their coffee. Having overheard the ladies talking, she said, "I didn't mean to eavesdrop, but It sounds like you two have been friends a long time. How did you meet?" "Just like this," Gina replied. "She poured me a cup of coffee at a hotel diner in New York thirty years ago." "That's it," Vanessa said, "and that night, I invited you to a party."

A casual acquaintance in a diner can lead to a lifelong friendship. The person you met at the party could become the mother of your future children. The new friend you make on summer vacation might one day be the maid of honor at your wedding. Every moment you live in the present is magical. It holds the power to shape the rest of your life. Every well-lived moment in the present will give you precious memories of your past. Never underestimate the power you have right now! Go to the party. Go on the cruise. Be nice to the server who pours your coffee. She might be the person who impacts the trajectory of your life.

Family and friends are witnesses to our lives. We depend on them to celebrate with us and grieve with us. They are the thread that helps weave the past with the future. They balance us by offering different perspectives. They can reframe our stories so we come out as the hero when we feel like the villain. They all have their entrances and exits in our life stories. They are all characters in our individual narratives shaping how the plot evolves. What matters most is the story we tell ourselves.

We are each characters in others' stories as well. We have all played the parts of heroes and villains in someone's life. We have little control over how others cast us in their narrative. The story can be told from so many angles. Always show up as your authentic self. Be true to yourself despite the stories others tell about you.

In what setting does your story take place? Where in the world is it happening? When is it happening? This also dictates the choices we make and the options available to us. In your story, in your setting, was leaving even an option? Perhaps acceptance was the only choice you had. If you are repeatedly cast as the villain when you know yourself to be a hero, can you change the script? One way to get unstuck from the past is to move to a new location in the present. That might be the best way to rewrite the future. Let your character live in a place where they can thrive. Now write the rest of the story from there.

Right now, in the present, your plot is still evolving. How will you write the next chapter? What role are you playing and how will you develop your character? Are there characters in your life who need to make an exit? How will you change the set? Your character's peace and happiness depend on what you are willing to change, what you are willing to leave, and what you are ready to accept.

Chapter Five

Changing It

Charlie worked for the same company for twenty years. He had reasonable benefits and was paid a competitive salary, but he never felt appreciated by his employer. He was passed over for every promotion he applied for, yet his employee evaluation never reflected any reason he was not promoted.

In his personal life, Charlie had been divorced for four years. He stayed in the same community at the same job because the stability helped him feel secure. Many of his closest friends and family had moved to other cities. Charlie was bored and lonely. He felt stuck, trapped in his life, and didn't know how to change it. Ironically, Charlie stayed in his situation because stability helped him feel secure. This is so frequently the reason people avoid change. They think, "This feels awful, but I am familiar with it. What if doing something else would feel worse?"

Charlie talked on the phone to friends regularly. He shared with them how his job was not rewarding, how he felt lonely but didn't know how to meet anyone, and how he couldn't make any changes because he didn't want to lose his salary and benefits when he was about to pay off his mortgage. Friends would ask, "What do you want, Charlie?" Charlie would always reply with, "I don't know what I want." One day someone asked Charlie a different question. "Charlie, what would make you happy?" Happy? It had not occurred to Charlie to be happy. Was that even something one could ask for? Charlie had just settled for feeling secure.

That question prompted Charlie to give it more thought. What makes me happy? When have I felt happy? It was a real challenge for him to list five things that brought him happiness. Coffee! Charlie always looked forward to his morning and afternoon coffee, so he put that on the list. Sunshine! Charlie hated winter. It made him feel sad and depressed. Nature! Charlie loved the outdoors. Biking! Charlie had not been on a bicycle since his divorce. He and his wife often biked together. He had given it up because it made him think too much about her. He remembered how good he used to feel after a long bike ride. Travel! Charlie had not gone anywhere since his divorce. He wasn't afraid to travel alone, but he worried it would cause him even more loneliness if there was no one to share it with. Charlie had his five things: coffee, sunshine, nature, biking, and travel. He also wrote down what he already liked about his life—security and stability.

Within a few months, Charlie took some of the equity out of his house and purchased a used motor home. He bought a bicycle. He negotiated with his boss the option to work remotely. He could have already done that, but going to the office had given him a reason to get out of bed. He traveled the country. He visited friends. Along the way, he hiked and biked in state parks. He enjoyed meeting new people at campgrounds and making new friends. He was getting healthier and stronger from hiking and biking. He looked forward to each new day and continued enjoying his morning coffee. Charlie changed his life in ways that were very manageable when he made the decision to be happy. He gave up nothing that already mattered to him. He returned to his house after each adventure. He was even considering selling it and moving to a consistently warmer climate.

Feeling trapped or stuck reinforces our stagnation and inertia. It is a loop we must eject ourselves out of. Sometimes it takes something big to shake us up: a divorce, a death, a job loss. Sometimes we can shake it up on our own if we open our minds to the possibilities and options that have always been there. Are you making excuses to stay in a job, relationship, or community that no longer brings you happiness? What are you willing to do to get out of your trap? What would make you happy?

Our greatest potential for change lies within. We have more influence over ourselves and our immediate surroundings than the rest of the world. Start with yourself. So often, we wait on change from others. We use others as an excuse for our unhappiness. Instead of taking responsibility for ourselves, we blame others for our misery. There is something we want them to do so we can feel happy. We are each accountable for our own happiness.

Change is not always neat and easy. It does shake things up and others don't always like it. The people closest to us have likely gotten accustomed to the way we are. When we change our life, even in some small way, it can also bring about change in their lives. I have often observed that when the addict in the house decides to get sober, the spouse suddenly decides, "I'm out of here." She stayed through the drinking, the arrests, and the financial instability, but once he became clean, sober, and consistently employed, she would have none of it. Misery does love company. Friends and lovers can bond in misery and discover that the relationship no longer works when one of the individuals gets healthy. The other feels abandoned and betrayed. Even when we do better, make better choices, and have success, others may still disapprove and reject our happier selves.

Sometimes we are ready for one change, but it brings other changes we didn't feel prepared for. When a couple decides to divorce, they may be ready to end the marriage. This is the change they chose to make. It brings more change with it. There is a change in disposable income because each is living individually in their own household instead of sharing tone. There will be loss of friendships. Though friends might say they will not choose sides, they generally do. Some people love their in-laws and think of them as their own family. In the best of divorces, those relationships will still be different. Change can bring consequences that may seem too big to face, so some people decide staying stuck is more convenient.

Humans tend to want two things in life: stability and adventure. We sometimes choose consistent misery because it is stable and predictable. We can rely on it. It feels familiar, like home. We settle for vicarious adventures through television or social media. It is a depressing life, but it feels safe and secure.

Charlie is an excellent example of someone who found a way to make a few small changes in his life while keeping the things that brought him security. Sometimes a few simple tweaks are enough to make it better. We don't always have to change everything. Charlie also discovered that by making a few simple changes, his mind began to open to making even greater changes in his life. If our mind can go there, on some level, we want it. Just allowing himself to travel again opened Charlie's mind to the prospect of living elsewhere. Allowing himself to get back on the bicycle brought him more joy and better health.

Change begins with one small act of intention followed by another. This is how we transform our lives one day at a time. The actions you take today will become the rewards of your future. Is today the day you change your life for the better?

Chapter Six

Leaving It

Joann was the youngest of three. At forty-two, she had never married. She had a few partners in her life, but none of the relationships lasted. Her older sister was forty-eight, married, and had one child in college, and another had just graduated. Her older brother was fifty-two, married with three grown children and two grandchildren. Their dad died at age fifty-nine from a heart attack. Their mother never remarried. When their mom's health began to deteriorate, Joann's siblings suggested Joann move in to care for her. They all had families. Joann did not.

Joann was close to her dad but never got along with her mom. Her mom was verbally abusive to her dad, Joann, and her siblings. They mostly tolerated her but felt obligated to see to her care in later life. If Joann moved in with their mom, their mom could stay in her home, and all of them could spare the costs of paying for assisted living.

Joann didn't feel good about living with her mom, but she knew someone had to look out for her. She tried to see the bright side of this. She could lease her own home while she lived with her mom, and this would pay her mortgage. She could save more money and maybe retire earlier than planned. Maybe this would be an opportunity to make peace with her mom and have better memories of her when she was gone.

Once the decision was made, Joann found a tenant for her own home within a month. She packed her clothes and personal items and moved in to live with her mom. Her siblings gave her little assistance with the move but lots of praise and gratitude for stepping up to do what they determined they could not.

Initially, it all seemed to go well. Joann helped her mother in the morning before she left for work and then assisted her again in the evening before they went to bed. They seemed to be developing a routine. Her mom was eating better, and the house stayed cleaner. However, about two months in, Joann observed her mom becoming more demanding and treating her like she had treated her dad. She started to criticize Joann and make unkind comments about her being single, her weight, and how she dressed. When Joann asked her mom not to talk to her that way, she reminded Joann that she was her mother and Joann was in her house. She alleged that Joann only moved in to live off her because she couldn't be successful on her own. The harassment seemed to get worse with each passing week. Joann couldn't blame it on age or illness. Her mom had talked to her like this at other times in her life. It was easier to tolerate when she could leave and get away from her.

Joann called her sister to request that she come to stay with their mother for a week so she could have a break. "I can't do that," her sister said. Her husband had knee surgery coming up and he would need her at home to care for him. Joann called her brother. He had a big project at work that might require some travel and it wasn't a good time for him to be away. "I am really dying here," Joann said. "Can you at least pitch in some money so I can hire a sitter for her for a week?" "Really?" her brother asked. "You are living there rent-free. You are making money from leasing your own home. You know how mom is. What did you expect? We all have obligations, Joann."

Joann felt angry at her siblings for not helping her out. She also understood they had their own lives. She envied them for having good excuses not to do the thing she felt stuck with. She took a deep breath and decided to give it another try.

Nine months passed when Joann got a call from her tenant. "We have to break the lease," they said. One of them was being transferred for work and staying was not an option. They would be out by the end of the month. On the way home from work, Joann thought about how she would find another tenant. This couple had only been there nine months, but they paid the rent on time and had taken good care of her home. Could she get that lucky again?

When she walked into the house, the first words from her mom's mouth were, "You're late." "Only by thirty minutes," Joann replied. "There was an accident on the freeway. I got home as soon as I could." "You always have an excuse," her mom said. "You've always been a fuck-up, Joann. That's why no man will ever have you. You are a lot like your dad. Same fat ass and everything."

Joann choked back tears. She wanted to scream at her mother. She wanted to throw something at her. She wanted to hurt her mom like her mom had so often hurt her. How dare she say anything bad about her father. She took a deep breath and walked to her bedroom. She removed her suitcases from the closet and began to throw in her clothes. "What are you doing in there?" her mom yelled. Joann never bothered to answer her. She finished packing her things, took her bags to her car, and quietly drove away.

Even with our best intentions, there are those situations that are so unbearable we cannot bring ourselves to stay. Maybe we tried to change it, but nothing worked. Maybe we vowed to do something differently, but we did it, and that didn't help either. Sometimes leaving is our only option for freeing ourselves from the person, place, or thing destroying our peace.

Leaving involves both acceptance and change. We accept the situation for what it is and take action to do the next right thing for ourselves. We accept that if we stay, this is as good as it will ever be. Leaving is how we change it.

So often, we stay in misery out of obligation. Someone else has expectations of us and we fear disappointing them. We fear their judgment and criticism. We worry about what others will think if we put our happiness first. If these are your reasons for staying, you have surrendered your happiness to another. Joann tried to honor an obligation she felt to her mom, her dad, and her siblings. She shouldered this obligation because she had designed her life to have more personal freedom than her siblings did in theirs. They assumed that Joann had lots of time because she was single and had no family obligations. Joann felt guilty for enjoying her peaceful life, so she agreed to give it up.

Joann bargained with herself to do something she didn't want to do. She tried to find some personal benefit for subjecting herself to her mother's abuse. She tried to pretend it was financially advantageous to give up her peace and happiness for the benefit of others. Then she bargained with herself to stay there once the abuse intensified and no one else would come to her rescue. We do this to justify our reasons for staying in bad relationships, bad jobs, and every other unhappy situation we find ourselves in. We fear others will judge us as quitters, weak, or selfish if we do what makes us happy. We test our strength and endurance by staying in physically and psychologically torturous situations.

Every relationship that matters will endure some degree of conflict. Most of the time, we can navigate it, shake hands or hug, and move forward. However, there are those individuals with whom we consistently find ourselves in conflict. Being in their presence causes us to feel bad. They are disrespectful, argumentative, demanding, and sometimes even abusive. You know the difference between someone who is toxic and someone who is simply having a bad day. Toxic people have bad attitudes that do not change. On some days, they may be less toxic than others, but it will always get worse again.

Toxic people often have severe addictive or personality disorders for which they are not getting help. People with personality disorders generally blame everyone else for their behavior. They often have a diminished capacity for empathy. Change comes very slowly for them, if at all.

People with addictive disorders can improve with recovery and go on to live highly functional lives if they can stay sober. Often by the time they achieve sobriety, they have left a path of destruction behind them.

If you are in a relationship with a toxic person, you have two of the three options we have already discussed: you can leave it or accept it. You will never change a toxic person. If change happens, it will be their own choice. Leaving may not be an easy option if the person is your relative. Children of toxic parents have a difficult time individuating and leaving the toxic mother or father. The abuse and grooming of these children begins so early that the victimization is integrated into the child's sense of self. In adulthood, these individuals will likely choose partners with many of the same abusive and destructive qualities as the toxic parent. If you stay in a relationship with one of these people, you will never have a peaceful mind or peaceful life until the day they die.

The longer we stay, the harder it is to leave. We have grown our investment of time and money and worry we will never recoup it if we walk away. Leaving feels like starting over and we tell ourselves that means we failed. Think of it as starting something new. Don't attempt to recreate the same unhappy scenario somewhere else.

Leaving does not necessarily equate to abandonment. People often say they stay in bad marriages for the sake of their children. "I couldn't walk out on them." I agree that a good parent doesn't walk out on their children, but you are not married to your children. Your relationship with them is different from the relationship with your spouse. Raising your children in an unhappy home is not admirable. When the marriage cannot be repaired, divorce is a reasonable option for giving everyone a better chance at happiness.

Joann didn't abandon her mother. She rearranged her peaceful life with good intentions to help her mother age in place. When thrust back into the same abuse Joann experienced in childhood, she accepted that her mother's personality had not changed despite her debilitated health. The abuse felt as bad as it did when her mother was younger and physically strong. Joann explained to her siblings she was willing to negotiate other options of care for their mom, but she wasn't willing to sacrifice her own health and happiness.

Just as people can cause us to feel bad, so can places. Organizations can be dysfunctional too. This is often due to the personality styles of those in positions of power and leadership. Employees in these organizations are trying to keep their jobs. They may have little flexibility or power to provide customers with a better experience. Don't be afraid to change your cable company, physician, or insurance if you are not getting the service you seek. If they are not trying to keep your business, customer service is not important to them.

Work environments also take on a personality. Some are welcoming, fun environments, while others are hostile and disrespectful of employees. Labor laws can vary from state to state. There are some national protections from things like harassment and discrimination, but resolution comes at the cost of time, money, and emotional wellbeing. Since most of us need to work, don't spend your career at a place that makes you sick. Dreading or fearing your work environment is a sure sign you need to get out of there. A toxic workplace is more likely to change you than you are to change it. You can't change the environment, but you can change jobs.

Cities, towns, and neighborhoods can also be toxic places to live. Things like crime and pollution raise stress levels and negatively affect the quality of life. The prevalent political mindset may not be conducive to the well-being of specific demographics of people. The climate of that region might negatively affect your health and happiness. Leaving might just be the change you need.

We can leave in the present or we can prepare to leave in the future. Most of us don't walk out the door impulsively. We spend a lot of time thinking about it first. We try other things. Once we decide to leave, we begin to strategize our exit. We figure out the who, what, where, when, and how to transition from here to there. Who will help us through the transition? What do we need to take with us? Where will we go? When will be the day we make the change? How will we get there?

Chapter Seven

Accepting It!

Edwardo and Carlos met in college in the early 1980s. It was a difficult time to be gay and their Latin heritage did not make it easier. The world was becoming aware of AIDS and gay men were often targets of hate and fear. When they each came out to their Catholic families, both were disowned. The chosen family of men around them was dying off, but Edwardo and Carlos found strength in each other and vowed to always be by the other's side.

Though marriage was never a legal option for them, they had a ceremony and exchanged rings. They met with a lawyer to give each other their official powers of attorney. They listed each other as beneficiaries on bank accounts and life insurance. They took all the precautions they could to protect their relationship.

They bought a home together, traveled together, and despite the challenges they faced, they made a very good life for themselves. In 2013, at age fifty-four, Edwardo was diagnosed with pancreatic cancer and within a few months, he was gone. After thirty years with Edwardo by his side, Carlos found himself alone. He had no contact with his family. He felt lost and could not imagine life ever having meaning without Edwardo.

The hospital social worker had referred Carlos to a grief support group at a local hospice organization. Carlos attended and found the sessions helpful as he coped with the loss of Edwardo. In one session, while discussing the stages of grief, the counselor asked Carlos to share his thoughts on acceptance. "I know a lot about acceptance," Carlos said, "For most of my life, it has been my only choice. I accepted that I was gay when I realized I couldn't change it. I accepted that my family disowned me when I told them the truth. I accepted that my church considers me an abomination, unworthy of God's grace. I accepted that I lost so many of my brothers to AIDS very early in my life. I accept that I live in a country where after thirty years with the same person, it's determined that I still don't deserve the right to marry. I have accepted a lot in my life that I could not change. Edwardo's death is one more thing I can't change. What other choice do I have? With time I will accept this too, but it will not be easy. Of all my losses, this one hurts the most."

Death is the most obvious example of something we cannot change. Acceptance is our only option. Acceptance, however, is not just an option in this most extreme scenario. It is an option with each challenge we face. Carlos identified many things in his life he could not change. They all affected him directly, but they all involved other people. He would have changed them if he could, but he recognized and accepted the limits of his power.

The past must be accepted in all situations because we can't go back in time and undo it. In the present, acceptance might still be the only reasonable alternative we have. In the present, we can change our perception of the past so it brings us greater peace of mind, but even that does not come without acceptance of what is. Carlos had experienced many losses in his life: his family, his faith, his friends, and his hope for justice. He still found ways to achieve happiness by being with the person he loved. He and Edwardo still bought a home, they traveled, they exchanged wedding rings, and they worked within the laws that existed to try to protect their relationship. What they could not change, they found a way to accept. About that, he had no regrets.

In this story, we can judge Carlos as the victim because so many unfortunate things happened in his life. The people he trusted and loved turned their backs on him when he didn't live up to their expectations. Religious, legal, and political systems rejected him or limited his options for happiness. Ultimately, he lost the most important person in his life, the one for whom he had sacrificed everything else. We could also judge Carlos to be a hero because he fought for love and let nothing or no one stand in his way. He persevered against the odds and found a way to be happy with the one he loved. He navigated the obstacles in his path and maneuvered the system using the resources he was allowed access to. Although in the end he lost the most important person in his world, he felt proud he was able to honor his vow to Edwardo that they would always be together till death parted them. Whether we judge ourselves to be victims or heroes depends on our perspective. Which role would you rather play? What conclusions do you come to about yourself as victim? As hero? Which conclusions serve you best in the present and will have the greatest influence on the choices you will make in the future?

Even when leaving or change are options, acceptance should not be judged as a cop-out. It is also a viable option. Our individual lives are complex, and answers don't always come easily. Others might look at your life and offer advice about what you should do, but they aren't you. Hear them out because their advice could be the key to your solution, but ultimately the choice is yours.

Acceptance is a graceful surrender that might come quickly or evolve over time. It is the peaceful yield to reality often referred to as serenity. In that way, it is a change of the mind to a happier place despite the circumstances. One way to achieve acceptance is by lowering your expectations. We love life to be predictable. It helps us feel safe when we know what to expect. You might know that it takes thirty minutes to commute to work each morning, so you plan your morning schedule accordingly to be at work on time. Then one morning, there is an accident on the freeway. Traffic is blocked and rerouted. The thirty-minute commute now takes an hour. You arrive at work late and must go straight into your first meeting with no time to review your notes, go to the restroom, or grab your morning coffee. The whole day begins wrong, and it is hard to recover.

The expectation of the thirty-minute commute throws everything else out of synch. You didn't get the coffee that was part of your morning routine. You didn't have time to stop at the restroom and felt uncomfortable throughout the meeting. You didn't have time to review your notes, and now you appear unprepared. An accident on the freeway has ruined your morning peace. Imagine if it had been you in the accident, how much worse that could have been.

It is difficult to release our expectations of the world. So much out there we cannot control, yet we live as if life should be predictable. We arrive everywhere with expectations that often are not met. The waiter provided poor service at the restaurant you reserved for your anniversary. It rains on your wedding day. The cat throws up on the sofa just as the guests arrive. There is a world pandemic, and your fiftieth-birthday cruise is canceled.

Lowering expectations requires that we let go of assumptions. One of the most significant disruptions to peace is that something didn't go as we had assumed. This is a lot like lowering your expectations but taking it to a deeper level. We are taught that the world is orderly and reasonable. It isn't. There is chaos all around us. Imperfection is everywhere. Your best strategy is to control the chaos in your mind. Change in the world begins with change inside your head. When you live with fewer assumptions and expectations, you rely more on yourself than others. Remember that your greatest opportunity for control lies within.

Acceptance is easiest when we don't take life too seriously. Life isn't permanent and no one gets out alive. Your life is a blip in time. You are a tiny little speck unrecognizable in the vast universe. This is good news. Most likely, one hundred years from now, no one will know who you are. They won't give a damn what you wore, what you did, who you slept with, how you voted, or where you went to church. Everything you define yourself by today will not matter to anyone living one hundred years from now. This is good news because it means you don't have to overthink every breath you take. Relax and just enjoy today.

Over the days ahead, observe all the places where you had an expectation that others did not fulfill. When you can lower your expectations, you will discover that you are not so often disappointed in the world. Human error is common, and most people are not critical thinkers. They can't understand the big picture, so they don't take accountability for how their actions or lack of can negatively impact others. Lowering your expectations is one demonstration of acceptance.

Chapter Eight

Mastering Thoughts

Life is just a series of thoughts, one after another. The mind is always thinking. Second guessing. Questioning. Worrying. Trying to figure it out. Wanting to make it better. Wanting to solve a problem. Wanting to prevent a disaster. It is so difficult to stop our thoughts from taking a negative turn. Like a game of connecting the dots, one negative thought can lead to another down a rabbit hole of anger, sadness, or fear. All day long, everywhere we go, we manage our thoughts and emotions, trying not to veer off the peaceful path.

Perception is our unique perspective of the world based on our thoughts. We perceive the world through our five senses of taste, touch, sight, sound, and smell. We don't all agree on what we think tastes good. We like different genres of music. I think the temperature feels too cool, but you complain you are too warm. The smell of roses reminds me of funerals, but it makes you think about being in love. Just more perceptions and thoughts. Rarely are they right or wrong. They are just different.

Most of life is conceptual. It only has meaning because we believe it does. Maybe it isn't an original concept. Maybe it is one you inherited from someone else. It has been suggested that tradition is peer pressure from dead people. Perhaps you are living your life according to the opinions of people who have long been gone.

Richard Brodie, author of *Virus of the Mind; The New Science of the Meme*, discusses the concept of mind viruses that can infect our minds with unwanted conceptual programming. A mind virus is a thought that spreads from one host to another. Like the flu, mind viruses can be contagious when introduced to a vulnerable, susceptible host. They are the thoughts that get into our heads and influence how we believe, feel, and ultimately behave. They filter our perceptions and affect our judgment. Brodie emphasizes that when "you better understand how the mind works, you can better navigate through a world of increasingly subtle manipulation." This is an important aspect of developing and maintaining a peaceful mind.

Mind viruses are impossible to avoid because our whole experience of life is organized around them. Thoughts create and maintain governments, religions, and institutions. They create trends and fashion and are used to sell us everything from automobiles to lingerie. They can serve us well by creating coalitions to enhance civil rights, fund charities, and open our minds and hearts to compassion for those in need. They can ruin us by diminishing hope, fostering apathy, or inciting violence and destruction. They give structure and organization to concepts of both good and evil. A cleverly crafted mind virus can fool its host into believing the most heinous of acts is honorable and justified.

We arrive in life with existing paradigms, traditions, and beliefs that we are groomed to accept as facts. Some people can do this quite easily, while others might question or challenge the status quo. Thinking minds recreate, second guess, perfect, and change. A rigid mind has trouble accepting that there are alternatives and that not everyone shares the same perspective. It wants to cling to what it knows and avoid change. It says things like, "Back in my day . . ." It longs for the *good ole days* when life seemed simpler, but good and simple are judgments we make from our unique perspectives. They are just thoughts and opinions. Humans are self-centered in that way. We think everyone else should see it as we do. Others see it differently because they have a different experience of life. Even if they live in the same city and time in history, they might not judge their life as good or simple. They might be thinking different thoughts because they live from different perspectives.

This is the basis for conflict: Two or more people having different perceptions and insisting that the others see it their way. Unfortunately, there are those who capitalize on this conflict and use it to fuel malicious agendas. They reinforce the fear of change. They perpetuate the belief that there is one right way. They demonize those who recreate, second guess, question, and think different thoughts. It is hard to have a peaceful mind in a world so in love with war.

Fear of people, places, and things we don't understand is wired into our primitive brains. It is part of our drive to survive. Conquering what scares us (and sometimes killing it) gives us a feeling of power and safety. Fear sells. It wins votes. It gains momentum and wields power. This is why observing the thoughts that drive your emotions is so important. Are they truly yours or someone else's? Can you back them up with evidence, or are they anecdotal? How do your thoughts influence your options to change, leave, or accept the circumstances in your life? If you didn't have fearful thoughts, would you make a different choice? Is the fearful thought a fact, or is it a fantasy that results in a fearful feeling?

Couples seeking therapy often come because they perceive their thoughts to be in competition. They want to learn to communicate better and resolve conflict. When they learn how to listen to each other, they frequently discover that they are both right. From there, they can negotiate a reasonable solution.

Tina and Carl came to counseling to address their conflicts about money. They earned comparable incomes but had different values about spending and saving money. Tina believed money was to be enjoyed. She worked hard for her income and wanted to reward herself. She liked getting her nails done regularly because it made her feel pretty. She liked buying new things for their house because she wanted to feel proud of their home. She liked traveling and going on adventures with Carl because that made her feel alive. Carl believed money should be saved. He would frequently coach Tina on the difference between a need and a want. He preferred to put money aside and watch it accumulate. A large savings account made him feel secure. Postponing pleasure was his way of preparing for an earlier retirement. The therapist helped the couple see that their agendas were not competing. They were both right. Tina could not argue that saving money was a bad idea. Carl couldn't argue that they should wait till their sixties to have fun. They learned that they could negotiate how they managed money so there was a reserve for emergencies and opportunities for adventure. The couple enjoyed developing a budget that would meet both of their goals. They stopped arguing and began collaborating to help each other succeed.

This is also the case with civil unrest on a much larger scale. Toxic leaders use conflict to foster fear and indulge their followers' beliefs in scarcity. They encourage the *us versus them* mentality to manipulate large groups of people into believing they are in danger. Instead of uniting people to collaborate toward the common good, they polarize them by embellishing extreme scenarios and fantasies, provoking fear and hate. These destructive mind viruses impede our peace collectively and individually. They stand in our way to happiness.

When we trust too much in the opinions of others, we can be swayed to accept and justify anything. Humans are inclined to be followers. We are content to be told what to do and how to do it. This is part of our tribal mentality, an innate aspect of our survival instinct. A vulnerable population on the edge of evolution can fall victim to a powerful resister of change. Though it looks like nothing is ever improving, we humans continue to evolve. Becoming ever more civil and enlightened but against strong resistance to evolution. This is the struggle we experience individually and collectively when we are on the brink of change because we so often perceive change as scary. You must look within for happiness. You cannot control the minds of others, but you can control your own. The world is full of toxic people and places that we cannot individually change. Accepting this and limiting or preventing our exposure to them is one way to keep your mind at peace.

When I graduated from high school, my grandmother gave me a plaque that read, "To live your life in your own way, to reach the goals you have set for yourself, to dream the dreams that you want to dream—that is success." Those words have stayed with me, and I can't think of a better definition of success. One means to mastering your thoughts so you can maximize happiness is to measure your success against your own goals and dreams. Live your life on your terms.

We are individually motivated by different desires. With every choice we make, there are other options we must forfeit. If you choose fame, you forfeit privacy. If you choose to be in service to others, you forfeit wealth. Certainly, early in life, we have few choices. We are given what we are born into, and when we grow up, we can choose to keep it or leave it. Either way, there will be gains and losses. Not one of us has it all.

Most people assume that success is determined by money and material possessions. It is the metric many people use to measure their status in the world. The things you once couldn't live without eventually become obsolete. No matter how much wealth you accumulate, it will never be enough to buy your way out of death. You only get one life, why not spend it doing what you love? Peace comes when we live the life we want according to our own dreams and desires. That is the ultimate measure of success.

A sedentary mind will wither and atrophy. It needs to be stretched and challenged through healthy stimulation to keep it engaged. Boredom and loneliness can destroy happiness. Humans need a sense of purpose and meaning in life. You will likely not find this in endless hours in front of a television or on social media. Constant exposure to news programming is a definite peace-killer. There is no good news. Because the human brain is designed to always look for danger, we fixate on stories of looming disasters. The headlines are rarely promising. Good news does not equal good ratings for news programs or networks. It rarely goes viral. It must be emotionally provocative and sensational to keep us tuning in daily.

News programs reinforce our fears. We see how unsafe and dangerous the world can be, so we feel more anxious. Someone was shot at the supermarket. What if that happens to me? We see how unkind people can be, and we feel angry. Someone makes disparaging statements about our race, religion, and politics, and now we want to say something inflammatory as well. We see how unfortunate life can be, and we feel sad. When was the last time you watched a news network and felt happy? Television and social media can be entertaining and useful, but they are loaded with other's memes, and they feed our minds with thoughts that are not organic and do not incite peace.

Mindfulness is awareness of thoughts and examining their validity, origin, and influence on your life. They drive our emotions and ultimately impact our decisions and outcomes. Thoughts evolve into the beliefs that govern our actions. They determine how much time we spend thinking about the past or future and living in the present. They shape our choices to change, leave, or accept. Mastering your thoughts will positively affect mastering your emotions and drive you ever closer to your goal of a peaceful mind and life.

Chapter Nine

Mastering Emotions

"I've learned that people will forget what you said, people will forget what you did, but people will never forget how you made them feel."

Maya Angelou

While we are ultimately responsible for our own emotions, they can certainly be influenced by the words and actions of others. Most people will feel sad or angry when treated unkindly, but these are not your only options. Imagine feeling confident, even when others are being disrespectful or unkind. You might also feel proud you could walk away and possibly never return. Our emotional responses to the stimuli around us result from our individual conclusions about our situation. That is the definition of perception. What we conclude about ourselves at any given moment will influence what we feel and how we behave. The conclusions we reach result from thoughts about ourselves that are already running on autopilot in the background of our minds. Our emotions are like a personal barometer subjectively measuring the perceived climate around us. They are abstract concepts without any universal objective metric and should never be confused with facts.

Early in my career, I worked in a setting where I was part of a multidisciplinary treatment team of different health professionals treating patients in psychiatric crises. There was a nurse on the team that I just couldn't figure out. In the first few days of my employment, she was friendly and welcoming, eager to help orient me to the job. I felt welcomed in her company. Then there were times I would walk by her office and say hello, and she wouldn't even look up to acknowledge me. I felt confused and wondered if I had said something that offended her. When I phoned her office to ask her a question, she would answer with something that made no sense. I felt angry and thought she was being sarcastic or evasive. Then I would see her in the hallway, and she was all smiles, saying hello and wishing me a good day. What was with this woman? What kind of evil, gaslighting, manipulating, mind-fucking was she trying to get away with?

About my third week there, I spoke with one of the psychiatrists and asked, "What is the deal with Nurse Julie? Some days she is friendly, some days she ignores me when I speak to her, then there are other times where she gives me sarcastic responses to something I say or ask." He bursts into laughter. "I guess no one told you," he said. "Julie is hearing-impaired. She has hearing aids, but they don't work well. You didn't notice them because of her long hair. You need to have eye contact, or she just responds to the few words she hears. She is great at reading lips, but she must see you face to face." Then I felt foolish, ashamed, and embarrassed. I had judged her unkindly based on my emotions and not the facts. I had reached inaccurate conclusions about her, supported by a few experiences, but clearly without all the information. In one moment, my entire perception of Julie, my working relationship with her, and my comfort with my new job changed. We perceive the world with the information we have, which affects the conclusions we reach and the emotions we feel. When we get more information, it can change our perception completely and ultimately change our mood.

So many of our reactions to our environment are based on misperceptions due to insufficient information. The mind wants to find an answer, so it searches its files for other times it had similar feelings and projects that data onto the current situation. So many of our triggers are unconscious data the mind recorded in the past, the last time it felt this emotion. Just as the smell of roses makes one person think of romance and feel amorous, yet another thinks of funerals and feels sad. These are just thoughts evoking emotions and are unique from one person to another.

Five of the most reported emotions include anger, fear, sadness, happiness, and shame. These emotions are chemical reactions in the brain based on our perceptions of the stimuli around us and our conclusions about ourselves. Emotions and thoughts are frequently confused. Men tend to have more difficulty identifying emotions than women. Men are socialized not to acknowledge fear, so in the presence of a threat, men often report feeling anger. Men associate crying with sadness, and since men are also socialized not to cry, men have difficulty identifying when they feel sad. When you ask a man what he feels, he will often reply with what he thinks. When we can identify our emotions, we can decipher the valuable data they carry. By observing our emotions, we can contemplate the validity of our thoughts and choose actions that serve us with the best potential outcomes.

Anger is often a misunderstood emotion. It is a response to a perceived threat—physical or conceptual. Physical threats can potentially cause injury or endanger life, while conceptual threats are mostly perceived insults or attacks on our character or esteem. At its best, anger is like a peace-keeping warrior. It protects, defends, sets limits and boundaries, holds accountable, motivates, and rescues. It is a call to action to defend and protect. At its worst, anger can be reactive, impulsive, abusive, or even destructive.

You are likely familiar with the phrase "fight or flight." When presented with a threat, we will either fight it or run from it. Running does not equate to cowardice. It might be the most logical and reasonable response to the threat. Fighting might seem more noble and brave, but it could also bring more consequences. Anger is part of the fight or flight response innate in all of us.

The amygdala is a region of the brain associated with emotional processing and controls some of the most primal aspects of the brain. It is part of the limbic system, sometimes called the primitive brain. Anger is triggered in this region of the brain, potentially causing us to react aggressively to perceived threats. Anger's close cousin, fear, the flight response in the fight or flight mechanism, is also triggered in this region of the brain. These cousins protect us from threats in our environment and have some similar physiological traits. Both produce rapid heart rate and increased blood flow to prepare the body for action, fighting or running.

Fear is cautious, apprehensive, and skeptical, and it seeks to prevent threats to survival. It is a problem-solver. It has been described as the flip side of anger, but it rarely gets the same respect. However, it is equally necessary for survival. It is also a call to action that danger is looming and to get as far away from the danger as possible. Anxiety, as a variation of fear, is future-focused. It worries about what will happen next. It wants to prevent and eliminate future physical or conceptual threats. Fear is a present emotion based on a current perceived threat, while anxiety is often experienced as dread or anticipation of something yet to come. Often people with anxiety disorders can't even articulate why they feel anxious; it's free-floating, generalized. Anxiety is the experience of fear in the present based on a scary fantasy about the future.

Sadness grieves, despairs, and regrets. It has lost someone or something it treasured. It seeks hope. It, too, has experienced a threat and perceives it has lost. Unlike anger, sadness is less recognizable because it rarely commands attention. It isolates and withdraws. If it goes out, it goes quietly. It does not come on as impulsively as anger, and there is generally no urgent call to action.

Happiness is content, peaceful, joyful, confident, and secure. It has everything it needs. It knows when the time is right to leave. It is ready to make change when change is needed. It also has the serenity to accept those things over which it is powerless to change. Don't confuse happiness with euphoria, an exaggerated feeling of joy often induced by drugs or mania. Euphoria cannot be sustained over a long period of time, but happiness can. Happiness knows that life is imperfect. It accepts this and it trusts its ability to navigate it.

Shame is self-loathing and insecure. It is the result of verbal, sexual, mental, physical, or ritual abuse. It has concluded that it is not good enough, damaged, and unworthy. To make its way to happiness, it must take all three routes out of Hell, a few steps at a time, down each rough path of change, acceptance, and leaving behind. It must leave its abuser so the emotional bleeding can stop. It must work hard to change itself and see more clearly who it truly is. The abuser has projected onto it an image that is not reflective of reality. It must accept where it has been and what it has survived. The conclusions we come to about the horrible things that happen to us will influence the degree to which we feel shame. When the abused is a child, it is imperative that adults do not project onto that child their own shameful interpretations of the event. Children often look to parents to interpret for them things they do not understand. So much of the shame one carries in later life results from the projections of others.

Brandy was six years old when her thirteen-year-old male cousin, Colt showed her his penis and dared her to suck it. Brandy loved her cousin and trusted him. He pulled her in her wagon and gave her piggyback rides. He reassured her when they watched scary movies. Though Colt was taking advantage of her innocence, Brandy had no judgment of sucking his penis as good or bad.

However, when she told her mom what she had done, her mom's reaction was a clear indicator that this was not good. Her mom cried and became enraged. She phoned Colt's parents and demanded they do something about how Colt had "ruined" Brandy's life. She told Brandy that she could never see Colt again. She took Brandy to the doctor for a physical examination. She called the police, the Department of Children's Services, and other family members. For the next twelve months, six-year-old Brandy had to tell one adult after another that she stuck Colt's penis in her mouth. Each one looked back at her with shock, disbelief, and pity. She no longer saw Colt or her aunt and uncle at family events or holidays. Brandy felt shame about something she didn't even understand. She wondered why her life was "ruined," as her mom said it was. She felt scared she would never see Colt or her aunt and uncle again. Brandy wasn't carrying her own shame. She was carrying everyone else's. Yes, an intervention was needed to protect Brandy and Colt, but instead, everyone reacted without regard for how their words and behavior were affecting Brandy's thoughts and feelings about herself.

So often, this is the case when it comes to children. Passionate parents interpret their children's lives through the filters of their own insecurities, prejudices, and judgments. They then project these beliefs onto the child. Just watch the parents' behavior at a little league game or a children's pageant. Child therapists often state that one of the most difficult things about working with children is having to work with their parents. These children often seek therapy on their own as adults to heal the damage caused by those who were *advocating* for them in their childhood.

When feeling your emotions consider the thoughts that are influencing them. How did you reach the conclusions that are driving the emotions you feel? Are they truly your own or just projections of another onto you? Is there a different way to interpret your story that would bring you to a more adaptive conclusion that emotionally felt better? Do you have all the information, or are you simply reacting to a few pieces of the story? We make major life decisions based on both emotions and thoughts. Understanding our emotions as they relate to our thoughts is important if we are ever to master them.

Chapter Ten

Taking Action

When we experience unpleasant emotions or negative thoughts, we want to act on them. We want to relieve the emotional pain and mental anguish. We want to calm our mind so we can be at peace. We seek some activity that will make it better, fix the problem, and restore our happiness. Our actions can potentially improve the situation or make it worse. Sometimes doing nothing is the most reasonable approach of all. By doing a reality check in the present, you will reorient yourself to the only place in time where you have any power. Ask yourself if the thing occupying so much of your mental and emotional energy is even real. Is it happening right now, or are you worrying that it might happen? If it has already happened, then it can't be undone. Identify the options you have to make it better and restore your mind to peace.

When we take responsibility for our own happiness, we are proactive at creating peace and minimizing chaos. We have learned from our mistakes. We live defensively in the world, dodging frustration, avoiding drama, and truly minding our own business. How wonderful to not have to worry about anybody's shit but your own. Isn't that enough?

The right actions allow us to change our circumstances in a way that brings us happiness. We can act by gracefully leaving behind what no longer serves us and perhaps never did. We can also prepare ourselves to accept what we can't change or leave for whatever the reasons may be. The following suggestions will get you started on taking actions that will lead you to a peaceful life.

Do Everything with Intention:

When we live mindfully, we observe ourselves in every situation. We know what triggers us. We know what relaxes us. We know our strengths and the areas where we need to improve. We understand that we must be proactive in creating the circumstances that bring us happiness. Passively waiting for someone to hand it to us does not work. Happy people assert themselves in ways that bring them joy. They understand that chaos is all around them, and every day, they must maintain their peace within.

We often confuse happiness with euphoria. Euphoria is rarely generated through normal life experiences. The euphoria experienced by people with bipolar disorder when they are in a state of mania is followed by depression. The euphoria addicts experience from their drug of choice is followed by the crash. Strangely, we sometimes feel euphoric in relationships with lots of conflict and drama. Happiness is stable and consistent and doesn't have that crazy edge to it. There are no steep peaks or deep valleys—just a smooth and easy ride.

Each morning, determine three simple things you will do that day that will bring you joy. Examples are a morning yoga stretch, walking in the park, and having lunch with your best friend. Whatever you choose, choose it with the intention of enjoying it. At the end of the day, you will have experienced joy at least three times. You will also discover that joy is within your power, based on the things you like to do, the places you like to be, and the people whose company you like to keep. You manifest it for yourself. It can also be simple, inexpensive, achievable, and measurable. Seven days of joy three times a day is twenty-one joyous experiences in a week. Not bad, is it?

Be Yourself:

It sounds simple, but it is one of the hardest things to do. We have such a strong fear of rejection, yet we frequently reject ourselves. We judge ourselves more harshly than anyone. We focus on our imperfections and dismiss our strengths. We fear we are not good enough as we are, so we try to make ourselves appear better for others. We portray an image we think others would like. Constantly performing for the approval of others is exhausting and does not feel authentic.

Positive affirmations can seem hokey. Initially, it feels awkward to say kind things about ourselves because we fear being boastful, even when we are alone speaking to ourselves in the mirror. Right now, list all the positive things you like about yourself, your achievements, and the compliments you routinely get from others. Your positive affirmations are not lies. They are the truths that you have minimized or dismissed. They are the rest of the story you are not telling or leveraging. Identifying them right now at this moment is an action toward changing the beliefs you have about yourself. Imagine how much better you would feel about yourself one year from now if every day you identified the things you like about yourself and acknowledged the successes you had each day.

When others tell you who you should be, you tell them who you are. "I know who I am" is one of the most powerful affirmations you can ever proclaim. It will manifest integrity, boost your confidence, and allow you to individuate yourself from those who seek to manipulate you for their own gain. Accepting yourself will radically change your life. Once you have clarity about who you are, you can release the projections of others. There are places you will no longer go and people you will no longer see. You will have more time in your life to invest in the activities that bring you joy. This is the path to integrity.

Master Confidence:

Confident people accept themselves. They can be authentic because they have decided they have nothing to prove. They know who they are despite what anyone else thinks. Don't confuse confidence with arrogance. Arrogance is a defense. Arrogant people keep others at a distance so their inauthenticity will not be discovered. It is an illusion of superiority. Confident people are not afraid to be themselves. They live in the moment with an awareness of their own power in their life. They change what they can. They leave the places that don't align with their personal happiness, and they accept that they are not perfect and that not everyone likes them. They can be content with where they are. Their attention is turned within, focused on their own personal goals and desires. Confident people trust their ability to handle what life gives them.

Be Assertive:

This chapter is titled "Taking Action" for a reason. You must do something. Passivity in a chaotic world is submission to the chaos. Being assertive means we actively go after the things that bring us happiness while also being respectful of others and ourselves. People often confuse assertiveness with aggression. Aggression also goes after what it wants but without boundaries or respect for others. Aggression bullies, assertiveness defends and protects. Look them in the eye and tell them what you want.

Take Out the Trash:

You are likely already doing a lot of things you don't enjoy and hanging out with people you don't like. This is taking up space in your life where you could be experiencing joy. Trash is the discarded matter that no longer serves us. It can also include the thoughts in our heads. Even if you don't yet know what you will replace it with, removing it is an act of assertion that something better can now take its place. You know the sense of accomplishment you feel when you clean out the garage, the closet, or the refrigerator. The extra space feels liberating. Make space in your life for the joy you are about to give yourself.

Let It Go:

Taking no action is sometimes the best approach. Doing nothing seems irrational if we believe disaster is looming. Do your reality check. Is disaster really looming? Do you need to take any action, or can you save yourself some time and energy by simply walking away? I sometimes refer to this as the turd on the sidewalk. No one likes that it is there and it's not the best place for a turd to rest. If you pick it up and move it, you now have shit on your hands. If you kick it or step on it, you have shit on your shoe. Stepping over it or walking around are the better options. Letting go is often a reasonable approach for those things we cannot change. Use the information you have learned from experience to guide your future decisions should you ever find yourself in this situation again. Letting it go has also been described as detachment. Maybe we cared too much about something or someone. Maybe the person or the issue was more important to us than it was to anyone else.

Wait Three Days:

In the present moment, our emotions might drive our decisions more than our rational mind. Time really does have a way of fixing some things. Three days later, we can think more rationally. The emotional intensity might be less. We may have more factual information on which to base our decision. Most things don't require immediate action. Generally, we have more clarity on the third day.

Feed your Mind:

You are what you think. Everything you read, watch, and listen to will influence how you feel about yourself and everyone else. Remember, most of what we think is the *real world* is nothing more than the made-up fantasies of others. It can all change in a heartbeat. Step more deeply into yourself by feeding your mind with the things that bring you joy.

Tell Your Story from a Different Angle:

Not everyone who is exposed to a disastrous event will experience trauma. Trauma reactions are unique and are influenced by our individual perception of the experience and what we believe about our own power at that moment. Psychotherapy interventions focused on trauma resolution help the client reach new conclusions about their experience.

Take a situation in your life that is causing you distress. Write about the situation as though you are the victim. Explain how you were disrespected, betrayed, deceived, and treated unfairly. Write about the outcome and how the victimization will negatively impact you for years to come. Now write about the same situation from the perspective of the hero. Explain how you overcame, persevered, and maintained your integrity despite the circumstances. As a hero, what was the outcome, and how will your triumph impact your life for years to come?

Fostering Hope:

Write down the names of five people in your life who are not part of your family of origin. Under each of those names, write the name of the person who introduced you or the place where you met. Then under that, write the name of the person who introduced you to that person or place. Keep going as far as you can remember. This exercise demonstrates how even random encounters can lead to new opportunities and how the choices we make in a single moment can directly influence our lives long into the future. Good things have likely been happening to you throughout your life. Sometimes the unpleasant things can overshadow them and cause us to feel despair.

Try Something New:

This is an exercise in facilitating change. If you are contemplating a change, try a test run first. There might be another way to approach the situation that would give you a better outcome. In my own life, I call these social experiments. Test your experiment a few times to be sure the outcome is consistent. Identify the thing you want to change. Outline the approach you have already taken and determine why it didn't work. Now outline a different approach and observe if this outcome is better.

Social experiments can feel awkward. We are testing a new behavior in a social setting. Perhaps you are typically passive and you want to experiment with being assertive. Perhaps you often perform the way you judge others expect and now you want to practice being yourself. It is easiest to test this in a setting where you have little to lose. If it is successful, work your way up to those relationships that feel riskier.

Do an Emotional Wash:

Imagine taking any situation in life and washing the emotion out of it and simply viewing it as data without any emotional reaction. This is especially useful for situations in which we feel anger. In these situations, we generally tell ourselves that someone is trying to threaten our happiness and it is necessary that we defend ourselves. We perceive so much of life as a personal attack. This is based on our exaggerated sense of relevance. The person who cuts you off on the freeway likely doesn't know you. Allow yourself to just see the situation as data without any associated emotion. Notice how your decisions in the moment will be different when you are not reacting emotionally.

Identify Your Own Projections:

Take fifteen minutes to sit in silence and simply observe others. Do this anywhere—at the airport, in the mall, or even on your patio or balcony. Humans are fascinating to watch. Imagine thought bubbles above their heads. What are their facial expressions and body language communicating? Remember that all of this is your own projection. Your judgments of others reflect your own beliefs and values.

Get Started:

Mastering a peaceful mind will give you a peaceful life. If you use the information in this book to do only one thing differently, you have already taken one step closer to happiness. Imagine how much happier you could be if you used all these tools every day. Right now, in the present, think of the changes you could make that will influence your happiness in the future. Identify what you could let go and leave behind you in the past where it belongs. Name what you must stop wrestling with and simply accept. There is your happiness plan. Implement it.

Chapter Eleven

The Role of Faith

The human mind has difficulty accepting that so much of life is beyond its control because it has evolved to seek solutions and explanations for everything. It despairs at the prospect of powerlessness. It scans its environment for answers. It searches its memory files of past experiences to compare this to that and thereby find a solution.

When the human mind can't make peace with reality, it creates fantasy to help it cope. It is comforted by thoughts of divine entities with answers and explanations not yet revealed. This helps the mind find peace by imagining protective entities with superior powers that humans lack. Help is on the way. The god, goddess, angel, etc., is in control. All the individual needs is faith. Faith allows us to trust that everything will be okay, even when we can't find a solution. It is one means by which we can cope with the painful realities of life.

Faith is hope that things will work out, and hope is a necessary aspect of mental health. As hopelessness increases, so does the risk of suicide. The mind cannot tolerate prolonged mental anguish. Faith is a tool of survival. One can have faith in anyone or anything, but the concept is frequently used to reference humans' faith in the divine.

Most people identify with the faith (religion) they were born into. The words and actions of the adults around a young child easily influence its mind. It can easily imagine Santa Claus and the Tooth Fairy. It is already inclined to create make-believe friends and bring stuffed animals and dolls to life. As the child matures, if the inherited deity mostly fits, they don't deconstruct. Doing so requires introspection and change that can be uncomfortable and often consequential. Even if they don't live it or completely understand it, it has imprinted on their identity, and they will continue to associate themselves with the deity they were given.

The human brain is designed for survival of the individual and the species. It wants desperately to change what frustrates and scares it. It can't accept its limitations, and in life, there are some catastrophes it cannot escape. The creative mind is always imagining how life could be better. So, the mind created deities to do what it could not. These divine creations had special powers the human projected onto them, powers the human wished it had for itself. Humans worshipped their deities with rituals of sacrifice, offerings, music, alcohol, tobacco, and money. To make these imaginary deities come to life, humans created images of their gods and goddesses. They painted, carved, and sculpted them so others could see their physical manifestation and reinforce their existence. They built large monuments and temples for the gods and goddesses to live in, and they visited these temples regularly.

We see common themes in gods and goddesses across time and cultures. Some disappeared when they fell out of favor, and new deities were imagined. When the projection ended, so did the god or goddess. Some were politically banned, bringing in a new deity that demanded to be worshipped. Today deities are still part of the fabric of life around the world. While we allegedly have the freedom to worship any of them or none, their presence in the minds of others makes them impossible to ignore. They are the basis for many laws that govern the lives of everyone, including the nonbelievers. Images of them appear everywhere, and they still demand gifts of money. Tobacco, alcohol, sacrificial virgins, and goats have mostly fallen out of favor.

We see similarities in deities represented in the minds of different cultures based on time and geography. Different projections by different cultures can be based on their unique desires for the same divine presence. In ancient Roman religion, Faunus was known as the rustic god of the forest. He is the equivalent of the Greek god Pan and comparable to the Medieval European god Woodwose, who is often referred to as "the wild man of the forest." Woodwose is similar to the mythological Green Man of the Forest, which is even depicted in the art of Christian churches and cathedrals in Scotland, Ireland, and England. Similar gods of the native peoples included the god Glooskap or Gluskabe. There were also earth goddesses such as Dheghom, Houtu the Chinese queen of the Earth, and the Greek Goddess Gaia. Gods and goddesses were believed to be born of other gods and goddesses, further examples of how humans project their own traits onto the deities they want to worship. Some humans believe they can personify the embodiment of their god or goddess. The Egyptian queen Cleopatra claimed to be the personification of the Egyptian goddess Isis.

Humans began transitioning from faith in multiple gods (polytheism) to only one god (monotheism) around the 14th century BCE under the rule of Egyptian King Akhenaten. He associated himself with the Sun God, (Aten) to consolidate power around himself. Monotheism became a method of control by forcing followers to place their faith in only one god. Those holding power would then declare what the god demanded and the consequences if you did not comply.

Theism (poly and mono) reveals a blending of stories of deities across human history. Jesus and the Greek god Dionysus were both born to virgins. There is an overlap of rituals on top of each other as gods and goddesses evolve and fade away. The rise of Christ on Easter is frequently associated with pre-Christ pagan rituals around fertility and being *born again* in the spring. Psychologists and anthropologists understand that archetypes like gods and goddesses can manifest around the world in different cultures unknown to each other. They are products of human thoughts and projections that tend to occur in every society throughout history. Collectively, they have been used to unite, motivate, or even manipulate large groups of people. Today humans reflect on most deities as myths wondering how anyone could have made these strange proclamations and others believed them. Given that there have been thousands of gods and goddesses throughout world history, atheists often joke that if you only believe in one of them, then you are 99 percent atheist as well.

One day while having lunch with a colleague, who identifies himself as a Christian therapist, he commented that most of his clients seek his services specifically because they also identify as Christian. Their religious faith is the basis of hope that gives them the psychological strength to persevere. He expressed surprise that they often misquote the Bible or blatantly make things up they claim they read in the Bible. "It's like they each have their own little religion and have decided to call it Christianity. Though they came to me for Christian counsel, they are often frustrated when I correct them about their interpretation or outright blasphemy." This highlights how humans manipulate religious faith to accommodate individually unique desires and beliefs. Our ancestors had the luxury of polytheism, with multiple deities for every occasion. Today's monotheistic gods are one-size-fits-all. Put it on and make it work.

Ethical therapists try to stay respectful of their client's faith. It is central to their belief system and their capacity for hope, and we therapists do our best to work within it. There are those occasions when we simply cannot help the client. Their god has trapped them in a mindset that will not allow them peace. They cannot accept, they cannot leave, and their god will not tolerate them changing their mind in a way that is more conducive to happiness.

Gayle Jordan is the executive director of Recovering from Religion, an international non-profit organization that helps people who have left religion, are in the process of leaving, or dealing with problems associated with theistic doubt or non-belief. Recovering from Religion offers support groups, individual peer support, and a telephone helpline. Gayle reports that she finds it easier to cope with life without believing in a supreme deity. Her personal experience of God was "arbitrary, unpredictable, and cruel." Today when life's journey brings tragedy, sorrow, or pain, she understands this is simply how the world functions.

Gayle states that questions about an afterlife often come up for those transitioning out of their religious faith. There can be grief associated with releasing the belief that you will one day be reunited with those you loved and lost and accepting that you will not actually see them again as you had once assumed. The consolation is to recognize the value of life in the present moment and the importance of maximizing relationships with the living so there will be nothing left unsaid or unresolved when death comes—no guilt or regrets. When you accept that death is final, you have a greater appreciation for your time with loved ones in the present.

For atheists, being without faith in a supreme deity is not synonymous with living without hope. There are so many wonderful things in life to experience and believe in: nature, art, music, love, family, friends, and even yourself. All these things and more can instill hope and offer meaning in life. Gayle states that life is less scary for her since she deconstructed her faith.

Prayer is thought, a meditation, a spell, a mantra, a hypnotic suggestion. Its power lies within. It can potentially manifest when it is a prayer for yourself. We also call this the power of positive thinking, the law of attraction, the secret. I once heard a former pastor proclaim that there is something more powerful than prayer—the power that resides within you. If your neighbor is hungry, you can pray they will get food, or you can take food to them. If your neighbor's house burns, you can pray they will find shelter, or you can invite them into your home. If you want to pass your history test, you can pray that you pass, or you can study. Humans have faith in the gods when they reach the limits of their ability to have faith in themselves.

Perhaps we are all gods and goddesses. We are each the creators of our own universe, per the thoughts we think and the actions we take. We have the power to change things, leave things, and simply accept them as they are. As God, what *miracles* are you willing to work in your own life? What *miracles* can you perform for those around you? Are you willing to be your own savior? What is the source of your faith, and how much faith do you have in yourself?

Chapter Twelve

Getting Help

Help can come from anywhere. A stranger's kind words or actions can turn your whole day around. We have that influence in each other's lives. So far, this book has examined how our perception of our circumstances directly impacts how we feel and behave. However, a self-help book about happiness will not fix everything. Maybe you have read several books, applied the concepts, and still, you find yourself feeling unhappy and struggling to cope. If so, it's time to seek professional help.

Mental health is as important as physical health. One influences the other. Like physical health, mental health is an afterthought for many people. Humans generally don't have a wellness mindset. We don't hold ourselves accountable for how we physically and mentally abuse our minds and bodies and make ourselves sick. We push the limits and then seek help when we are ill. There are also those illnesses that are indigenous. Like certain physical illnesses, we can also be genetically predisposed to mental illness.

There has long been a stigma associated with utilizing mental health services. Though some people do die from mental illness, most don't. Since you can usually live without help, many people don't take their mental health seriously. When one is struggling with mental illness, it can affect everyone around them. It impairs the quality of their work, relationships, and life in general. Your untreated mental illness can even put the lives of others at risk. If you or someone you know needs help, don't put it off. Start somewhere.

There are different disciplines of mental health providers, which can confuse the average person who doesn't know the difference between a psychiatrist and a psychologist. When mental health providers are portrayed in the movies, they always fall into one of these two categories, and sometimes the writers don't know the difference either. Ironically, most licensed mental health providers are neither psychiatrists nor psychologists. They are more likely to identify as clinical social workers, marriage and family therapists, or mental health counselors.

Psychotherapy is a generic term referencing the different clinical theories and interventions used to help mental health clients heal. A psychotherapist is an individual from any discipline licensed to practice as a mental health provider. This includes social workers, marriage and family therapists, mental health counselors, psychologists, and psychiatrists. Some states have unique exceptions for other disciplines too. Those eligible for a license to practice psychotherapy are graduates of accredited universities and accountable to state, federal, and professional regulations as well as ethical standards of conduct. They must demonstrate competency on a licensing exam and be closely supervised during their first few years of practice. They must renew their licenses regularly and meet the requirements for continuing education. All of them are licensed by the health boards in their state. They may individually have additional certifications based on their specializations of care. You can also be licensed in any of these disciplines and gainfully employed, yet not provide any psychotherapy services directly. Some licensed mental health providers are educators, trainers, program directors, and researchers, and may even be employed in business administration or marketing because of their unique training and skills.

A psychiatrist is a medical doctor who specializes in psychiatric medicine. Their primary treatment modality is psychotropic medication. Most provide limited psychotherapy, if any. Some people have both a psychotherapist and a psychiatrist. In some states, physician assistants and nurse practitioners can also prescribe psychotropic medications and be independent specialists in psychiatric care. Even your primary care physician can prescribe and manage your psychotropic medication if they are willing to take on this additional role in your healthcare. A psychiatrist is preferred when your mental health needs are complex, life-threatening, or have not been successfully resolved with psychotherapy alone.

Windle Morgan is a psychiatric nurse practitioner in Nashville, Tennessee. He is the president and co-founder of Novo Healthcare, an organization providing psychiatric services to adults, children, and adolescents. Mr. Morgan identifies three things that can prompt someone to seek psychiatric care: self-determination, encouragement from family or employer, and community intervention or referral. It is best when we recognize we need help and seek it at our own will. Sometimes others notice changes in us before we notice or admit them ourselves. A family member or coworker who is with us every day might recognize changes in mood or behavior. When people we trust express concern, their gentle encouragement might prompt us to consult a mental health provider if we have been in denial or ambivalent about getting help. Mr. Morgan states, "It is hardest to engage patients referred by third parties," such as emergency rooms or legal authorities. If the patient needs intervention by police or emergency medicine, they have allowed their situation to deteriorate to critical status. Their denial of psychiatric impairment is so severe that they are unlikely to stay engaged with outpatient maintenance regimens that include medication and follow-up appointments.

Psychotherapy without medication is generally sufficient for treating most mental health problems. While psychotherapy is increasingly accepted, many people resist it because they don't understand it. They worry they will be judged or labeled. They are ashamed to be vulnerable, even in the therapist's presence. People sometimes avoid psychotherapy because they believe one must be "crazy" to need these services but that is a myth. Crazy people don't get much benefit from psychotherapy. They must first be stabilized by medication or hospitalization before they can be insightful and cognizant enough to process and learn.

Like other aspects of health care, patient privacy and confidentiality are protected in most circumstances for all levels of mental health treatment.

In psychotherapy, clients learn new skills for managing and navigating life's challenges. They learn how to examine and change maladaptive beliefs, thereby changing uncomfortable emotions as well. Doing so leads to different actions and, ultimately, different outcomes. The skills you learn in psychotherapy can last a lifetime. It is one of the few investments you can make in yourself that will have positive benefits for you and your family for years to come.

Increasingly people are utilizing coaches to make important life and relationship changes. Coaches motivate, teach, encourage, and support their clients toward making the desired changes in their life. They don't diagnose mental disorders, but they might be utilized as a part of a wellness treatment team to help clients manage their mental illnesses. Sometimes they have a specific specialization, such as behavior modification or addiction recovery. Some psychotherapists market themselves as coaches because they believe coaching is more descriptive of their work with clients.

In recent years there have been some bizarre and radical laws in more conservative US states that impact how mental health providers deliver health care services. Since coaches are not licensed, they are not regulated under state laws that can be discriminatory in delivering professional services. Coaches are not limited to specific geographical jurisdictions and can easily practice across state lines. This is convenient for clients who travel or have homes in multiple locations. Since coaching is not regulated, anyone can claim the title with little or no expertise in what they claim to specialize in. This is the downside. Don't hire them just because they tell you they are a coach. Ask for their credentials. What experience do they have? Has someone recommended them? Can they provide you with recommendations from other clients?

Whether you hire a therapist or a coach, getting a recommendation from someone you trust who knows them is always a good idea. If you are searching on your own, take a close look at their experience and credentials. Some people search for providers solely based on who is the cheapest and who takes their insurance. Insurance will not pay for coaches if they are not also licensed as healthcare providers. Many psychotherapists don't take insurance because they cannot financially afford to. Participation in insurance networks requires providers to negotiate and significantly reduce their fees. They must then increase the volume of patients they see to balance the financial loss. While a physician might see forty or more patients a day, a psychotherapist rarely sees more than six to eight. The typical psychotherapy session is forty-five minutes. Cutting fees by as much as seventy-five percent to accept insurance will put most therapists out of business.

Below are some common resources for finding qualified mental health providers:

Psychology Today maintains a database of providers that can be easily sorted and researched based on multiple qualities that might be important to the mental health consumer. This includes specialization, discipline, and cost of services.

https://www.psychologytoday.com/us

The **Secular Therapy Project** maintains a database of mental health providers who practice from a science-based model without subjecting the client to unwanted religious practices. It might seem obvious that health providers operate from a science model. While they are trained that way, some clinicians don't separate their clinical training from their religious orientation, which is especially common in more conservative regions of the country.

https://www.seculartherapy.org/

The **American Association of Sexuality Educators, Counselors, and Therapists** provides a directory of clinicians uniquely specializing in sex therapy. This is a valuable resource since most American healthcare providers receive no training in basic human sexuality. Sex therapists are psychotherapists who also have specialized training in sexology, the science of sexuality.

https://www.aasect.org/

Chapter Thirteen

Take Aways

You are the CEO in your own life.

You are accountable for your own happiness.

The key to your happiness lies within.

Material possessions bring short-term happiness. Landfills and thrift stores are full of things you once thought you couldn't live without.

Collectively, human behavior does not change. Humankind has made the same mistakes repeatedly across history. Humans are innately driven by greed, anger, desire, and power. Understanding and accepting this will help you achieve more realistic expectations of yourself and others.

We are each our own worst enemy. We harm ourselves routinely with negative self-talk, abuse of our bodies, and sabotaging our own paths to happiness.

Much of what you believe is not your original thought. It is the opinions and beliefs you inherited from someone else.

It is thought that runs the world and dictates the actions that lead to our happiness or misery. Thoughts influence emotions which influence the choices we make and the actions we take.

The human brain is designed for survival.

The anxious mind does not differentiate between physical and conceptual threats.

Life's problems fall within three places in time: the past, the present, or the future.

The past has already happened and is not changeable. In the present, you can change your attitude about the past and then come to new conclusions.

The past is a memory. The future is a fantasy. Both are thoughts. The present is where change happens. Every new moment is an opportunity to think a better thought, choose a better action, and change the trajectory of your future.

Staying stuck in the past can lead to depression.

Worrying about the future can lead to anxiety.

Making peace with the past will change how you live in the present.

How you live today will influence your potential for happiness tomorrow.

Every well-lived moment in the present will become the precious memories of your past.

In every moment, we make the best possible decisions based on the information and resources we have available to us in that moment. The choices you made in the past were based on your best judgment then. If faced with the same circumstances today, you might make a different choice.

The time it takes to heal your mind is entirely up to you. Begin when you are ready.

In all of life's challenges, we have three options; change it, leave it, or accept it.

If you change it and it does not work out, you can always change it again.

Change begins with one small intentional step followed by another.

Change is easiest when we don't have to rely on anyone else.

It is okay if you no longer want the thing you once chose.

Our greatest potential for change lies close in because we have more influence over ourselves and our immediate surroundings than we have over the rest of the world.

Even positive changes in your life will encounter resistance from those closest to you.

Some things cannot be changed or left. They can only be accepted.

Acceptance is a viable option.

To have one thing, something else must be forfeited. No one has it all.

Humans have a tenacious capacity for tolerating misery, and this is part of our innate drive for survival.

Humans will stay stuck in misery because it is predictable and familiar.

You are not obligated to be miserable.

We perceive the world through our five senses. Sensory perception is subjective.

Our perceptions drive our emotions.

Emotions are also subjective and cannot be universally quantified.

Don't confuse what you feel with what you think.

Feelings are not facts. Thoughts are not necessarily facts. Sometimes they are just perceptions, projections, or beliefs. Don't believe everything you think.

Conflict occurs when we make incorrect assumptions (thoughts) about others when they are not living up to our expectations (more thoughts).

Imperfection is ubiquitous. Expectations and assumptions set us up for disappointment.

Peace and happiness are judgments based on our perception.

Don't look to others to define you. Define yourself.

We are each characters in someone else's story. We can't control what they project onto us or if they cast us as a villain or a hero. Always know what character you are playing in your own story and play your part well.

Regardless of your past story, the plot can always change. You are writing the present in every moment. How will you write your story today and how will that influence the final chapters of your life?

In the stories you tell about yourself, do you take the role of victim or hero? If you tell the same story from the opposite perspective, does it change the way you think and feel?

Don't bargain away your joy.

Leaving requires both acceptance and change.

The longer you stay, the more difficult it will be to leave.

Conflict is a normal aspect of every meaningful relationship. Toxic abuse is not. Toxic people and places rarely change. Sometimes our only chance for happiness is to leave.

Don't take life too seriously. It isn't permanent and no one has ever gotten out alive.

Over one hundred years from now, it is unlikely that anyone will know who you are. Your significance and relevance are minimal and fleeting. So why not have some fun?

You are the only person who will ever be living your life.

Life is mostly comprised of thoughts. Overthinking life will compromise your joy.

Perception is thought that is unique to you even when it might be shared by others. Not everyone will share your perception. Some people are thinking different thoughts.

Your opinion matters mostly to you.

Many of your thoughts were inherited from people who died a long time ago. This has been referred to as "peer pressure from dead people."

Thoughts can spread like viruses. They seek a vulnerable host who will also spread them to others.

Humans are innately attracted to stories about threats to their safety. Advertisers use this knowledge to sell products. Politicians use it to win votes. Scam artists use it to steal money.

In childhood, we are each groomed to live according to someone else's thoughts.

Most people are comfortable living according to the thoughts of others.

Fear is the innate experience of a perceived threat. It is an emotion influenced by thought.

We are ultimately responsible for our own emotions.

Feelings result from the conclusions we reach about ourselves based on our individual perceptions of our circumstances.

Anger is a normal emotion. It is a call to action when a threat is perceived. Anger's mission is to protect, defend, advocate, and motivate.

Fear is a normal emotion. It also perceives threat. To better understand your anger, you must also understand your fear.

Anxiety is fear of something that has not yet happened and rarely ever does.

Euphoria cannot be sustained and is often an unnatural and abnormal state of being.

Shame results from abuse—verbal, physical, emotional, sexual, or ritual.

We frequently make decisions based on emotion instead of reason. It is why we often judge another and ask, "What were they thinking?" They were not thinking. They were feeling.

Live assertively with intention.

To accept yourself as you are is a sign of confidence.

Confidence results from knowing and accepting yourself.

Be yourself.

Get rid of what no longer serves you.

Try something new. Then assess the outcome.

Let go of what you cannot change. Sometimes nothing is all you have to do.

Faith is hope that things will improve. It is an innate aspect of human survival.

Belief in divine entities is one form of faith common for humans throughout world history and across every culture.

The gods we have faith in are the projections of our thoughts.

Be intentional with every action. Know your motivation and the outcome you are seeking.

If you can identify one simple thing you can enjoy each day, then you will experience joy each day of your life. Now go for two things. Three.

Success is a judgment. There is no universal metric. You get to set your own goals and define your own success.

Happiness is one measure of success.

Learn from your successes and your failures.

Let go of the people, places, and things that no longer bring you joy.

Wait three days and see how time influences what you think and feel.

Don't pollute your mind with toxic people, places, or things. If it causes you anger, sadness, or fear, it is potentially toxic.

Random encounters can lead to new opportunities. Every moment is potentially magical.

Experiment with something new.

In a situation where you experience emotional distress, imagine extracting the emotion from the situation and simply observe the data. When you extract your emotional reaction, does the conflict, situation, or problem now seem more manageable?

Stay mindful of your projections. Most of life is subjective. How does your attitude influence your perception?

Define your happiness plan and decide when you will begin.

Resources

Brodie, Richard. *Virus of the Mind : The New Science of the Meme*. Carlsbad, Calif.: Hay House, 2011.

About the Author

Steven Davidson, PhD, LCSW, is a psychotherapist and clinical sexologist in Fort Lauderdale, Florida. He has over thirty years of experience helping individuals and couples achieve personal and relationship happiness. He is also the author of *Sexual Integrity: Finding the Courage to Be Yourself.*

You can reach Dr. Davidson through his websites at drstevendavidson.com or sexualintegritycoach.com

Special Thanks To

Gayle Jordan
Windle Morgan
Michael Vignogna

www.ingramcontent.com/pod-product-compliance
Lightning Source LLC
Chambersburg PA
CBHW071008080526
44587CB00015B/2388